EXPLORING A CASTLE

Brian Davison and Peter Dennis

Kingfisher Books

Educational advisers: Mary Jane Drummond,
Cambridge Institute of Education, Cambridge
Iris Walkinshaw, Headteacher, Rushmore Infants School, London

Kingfisher Books, Grisewood & Dempsey Ltd,
Elsley House, 24–30 Great Titchfield Street,
London W1P 7AD

This reformatted edition first published in 1992
by Kingfisher Books
10 9 8 7 6 5 4 3 2 1

Originally published in 1987 as *Stepping Stones 456: Looking at a Castle*
by Kingfisher Books

British Library Cataloguing in Publication Data
A catalogue record for this book is available
from the British Library.

ISBN: 0 86272 960 2

Edited by Vanessa Clarke
Designed by Ben White
Cover designed by Pinpoint Design Company
Phototypeset by Southern Positives and Negatives (SPAN),
Lingfield, Surrey
Printed and bound in Portugal

Contents

The Old Castle

The castle is old. Older than Gran and Grandad. Older than your town. No one lives in the castle any more. There is no glass in the windows, the walls are broken and all the roofs have fallen in.

In the Middle Ages

Hundreds of years ago, during the Middle Ages, the castle was new. It was built by a rich man, the Lord of the castle. He built it to protect his family, his servants and his friends. In times of war, they rushed into the castle and stayed safely behind the closed doors and strong walls.

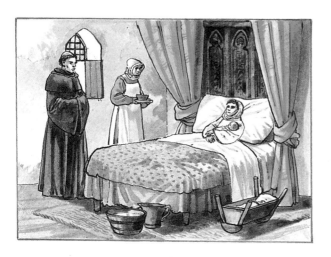

The castle was the Lord's home. Inside the
walls he and his family could live as
they pleased. In times of peace, the castle
was full of music and laughter. It was a
happy place to live in.

Outside the Castle Walls

Now we are closer, the old castle looks even bigger and more forbidding. How did people attack it in the Middle Ages when it was new? Where would we start?

Would we climb over the walls with a ladder? Dig a hole under the walls? Or force our way through the front door?

Getting In

Bridge over ditch

The way into the castle had to be strong enough to stop the enemy from getting in. Around the castle was a deep ditch. In the Middle Ages the bridge over the ditch could be lifted up to stop anyone crossing it. In front of the door there were grooves in the walls. A portcullis slid down the grooves to make a gate. Then came the doors. The holes in the walls behind them were for wooden bars which kept the doors closed.

Portcullis grooves

Door

First fill in the ditch...

...then use the battering ram...

...but what about the portcullis?

Getting in would not be easy. The people inside would try to stop the enemy soldiers by shooting arrows at them and by dropping heavy stones on their heads. Many of the soldiers would be killed.

11

Up On the Battlements

Nowadays the old castle is
easy to get into. Over the
bridge, through the doors, and
up the twisting stairs we go,
up to the top of the tower.
Now we must defend the castle.
But how can we shoot at the
enemy without leaning out and
getting shot ourselves?

We could hide behind the battlements, and shoot through the arrow-loops.

Wooden hourd

We could push beams through those holes below the arrow-loops and build a wooden hourd.

Arrow-loop

Built for Defence

There were many wars in the Middle Ages and soldiers found more and more ways to get into castles. So the castle people built several lines of walls and towers, one inside another. Then the defenders could retreat from one line to the next if the enemy forced them back. Right in the middle was the biggest and safest building of all. This was the Lord's keep.

If enemy soldiers got over these walls, where would we go next?

The Lord's Keep

Inside the Keep

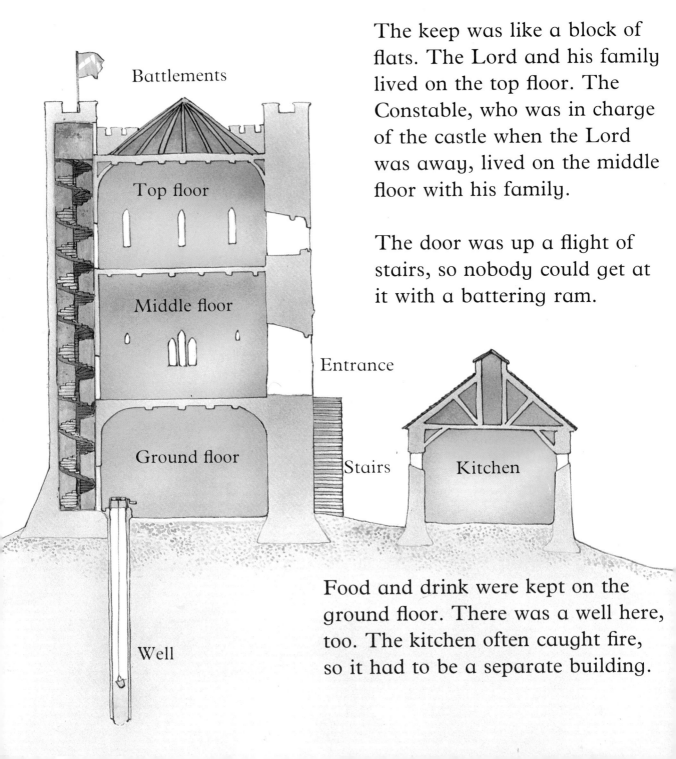

Battlements

Top floor

Middle floor

Ground floor

Well

Entrance

Stairs

Kitchen

The keep was like a block of flats. The Lord and his family lived on the top floor. The Constable, who was in charge of the castle when the Lord was away, lived on the middle floor with his family.

The door was up a flight of stairs, so nobody could get at it with a battering ram.

Food and drink were kept on the ground floor. There was a well here, too. The kitchen often caught fire, so it had to be a separate building.

In the keep the walls were made of stone, but the floors were made of wood. In the Middle Ages there were rugs and rush mats on the floors. The walls were painted white with beautiful cloth and tapestries hanging on them. The toilets were small rooms with chutes going down inside the walls to smelly pits filled with straw. They had to be emptied by hand.

Living in the Keep

It's morning! The servants open the shutters, light the fire and pull back the bed curtains. The servants sleep in the same room as the Lord and his wife, the Lady. During the day they push their beds under the Lord's bed. For breakfast, there is beer to drink, and bread with cold meat or fish.

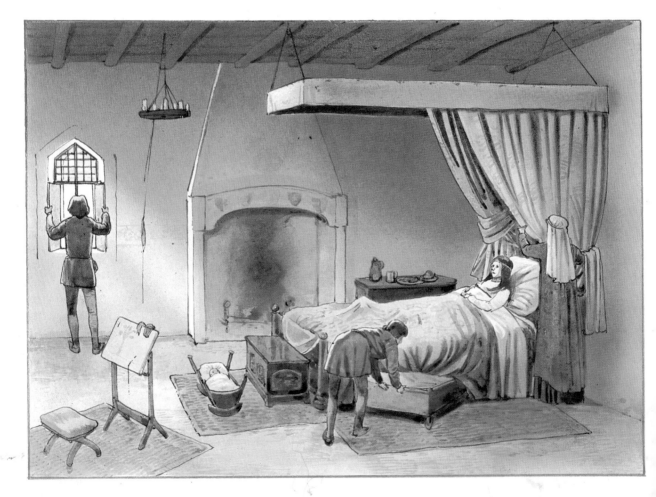

Every morning after breakfast, the Lord goes to his private chapel. The chapel is the most beautiful room in the keep because the castle-builders decorated it for God. The Lord keeps all his business papers and money in the chapel since it is the most private place in the whole castle.

The Kitchen and Great Hall

After prayers, the Lord and Lady often go
hunting. Sometimes the Lord meets other Lords
in the Great Hall to discuss politics or to plan
for the next war. The kitchen servants spend
the day getting dinner ready. The fireplaces
have to be big enough to roast a pig or a cow.
There are no freezers, so in winter all the meat
and fish is salted to keep it from going bad.

Late in the afternoon, everyone goes to the Great Hall for dinner.

The food is carried in to the sound of trumpets. There are three courses, but each course has many different sorts of food: roast swan, fish pie, duckling stuffed with nuts, castles made out of marzipan. The food is put on thick slices of bread instead of plates.

Castle People

The castle is like a small town. More than one hundred people work and live there but only a few are women. Nearly all the work in the castle is done by men.

Horses, Hounds and Hawks

As well as people, the castle is full of horses, hounds and hawks. The horses are the most important animals. Castle people could not manage without them. Horses carry the Lord and Lady when they go hunting, and their knights when they go into battle. Messengers on horseback carry all the Lord's letters.

Down in the castle yard is a building called the Mews where the hawks are kept. The Lord keeps several hawks: he likes to watch them catch their prey in mid-air. It takes a long time to train a hawk so the Falconer takes good care of them.

Nobody takes good care of the prisoner in the dungeon unless he is rich and can pay a ransom.

Types of Castles

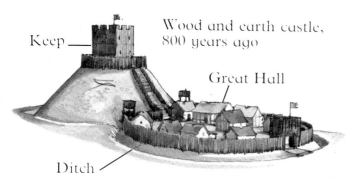

Wood and earth castle, 800 years ago

Keep

Great Hall

Ditch

The Middle Ages lasted for four hundred years. During that time people thought of new ways to stop the enemy getting in. So they built different types of castles.

Stone castle, 700 years ago

Keep

Ditch

The first castles were built of wood and earth. Castles like this were cheap and easy to build. Later, castles were built of stone. It took longer and it was more expensive to build stone castles but they were much stronger and much safer.

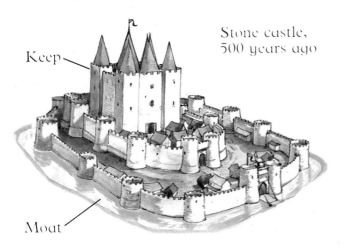

Stone castle, 500 years ago

Keep

Moat

There were all sorts of stone castles. Some had round towers and some had square towers. Some had water in their ditches. Every one was a different shape and size.

A poor Lord's castle

Lords wanted large castles to
show how important they were.
But not every Lord could
afford a big castle with lots of
walls and towers.

A rich Lord's castle

A King's castle

The End of the Castles

Gradually, people found new ways of attacking castles. They invented new weapons. The most important new weapon was the gun. With a really big gun soldiers could knock down the walls and towers. Then the castle people had to surrender.

It wasn't just ways of attacking castles that changed. The Lords got better at settling arguments without fighting each other so often. Lords and Ladies no longer needed castles. They wanted to live in more comfortable houses with big windows and private rooms.

When the Lords and Ladies moved away to their new comfortable houses the old castles were left empty and deserted. Nobody took care of them. Gradually, people forgot about them.

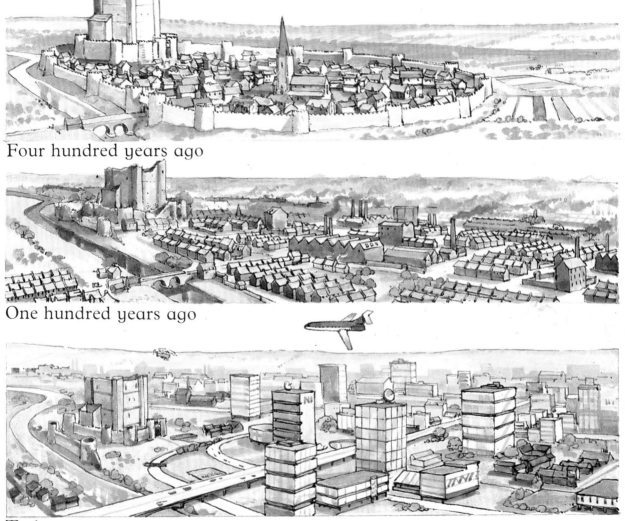

Four hundred years ago

One hundred years ago

Today

The Castle Today

Today the old castle sits on its hill. It's just an old ruin, empty and quiet. The only voices are our own, as we explore the towers and passages. The furniture, the tapestries on the walls, and the castle people themselves – they have all vanished.

This stone looks like the ones we saw in the windows of the keep.

But we can bring them back. We can look at the Great Hall, the Lord's keep, the empty fireplaces in the kitchens. We can touch the fallen stones from the Chapel windows. We can imagine the horses and the hawks, and all the castle people in their colourful clothes. Long ago, this was their home.

Index

How to find castles

There are hundreds of castles you can visit. There may be one near you. Ask at your Library or Museum, or write to these addresses and ask for a list of castles. Remember to enclose a big envelope with your address and a stamp on it.

England
English Heritage
Fortress House
23 Saville Row
London W1X 1AB

Wales
CADW
Brunel House
2 Fitzalan Road
Cardiff CF2 1UY

Scotland
Historic Scotland
20 Brandon Street
Edinburgh EH3 5RA

Northern Ireland
DOE
Stormont
Belfast
BT4 3SS